Lin Wellford's

Painted Garden Art
anyone can do

ArtStone PRESS

D1312471

Acknowledgments—No book happens in a vacuum. I am grateful for the input and encouragement I receive from readers and friends. Special thanks to Elaine Floyd of EFG Publishing, Inc., who generously shares her vast book design and marketing expertise, and to Sally Ann Finnegan, friend, colleague, photographer, stylist, and original "Sturdy Girl."

Other Books by Lin Wellford:
Rock Painting Fun for Everyone! (ArtStone Press, 2006)
Painting Zoo Animals on Rocks, (North Light Books, 2004)
Painting on Rocks for Kids, (North Light Books, 2002)
Painting Pets on Rocks, (North Light Books, 2000)
Painting Flowers on Rocks, (North Light Books, 1999)
Painting More Animals on Rocks, (North Light Books, 1998)
Painting Houses, Cottages and Towns on Rocks, (North Light Books, 1996)
The Art of Painting Animals on Rocks, (North Light Books, 1994)
    Video:
Paint Animals on Rocks with Lin Wellford Video, (ArtStone Press, 2000)

Published by: ArtStone Press
        9328 Highway 62 E.
        Green Forest, AR 72638
        SAN 850-010X

Printed and bound in the USA
10 9 8 7 6 5 4 3 2   07 08 09 10 11 12

Library of Congress Control Number: **2006910355**

Wellford, Lin
    Painted Garden Art Anyone Can Do/ Lin Wellford
ISBN-10: **0-9777065-1-6**
ISBN-13: **978-0-9777065-1-8**

Editors: Kristen Helams, Erika Kupfersberger, Skye Pifer
Cover Photography: Sally Finnegan
For more information on ArtStone Press books, visit www.ArtStonePress.com or
                www.LinWellford.com

Introduction

Have you ever thumbed through a gardening magazine and wished for the time and talent to make your own outdoor areas look that spectacular? The reality of gardening is that it is labor intensive and results are often unpredictable. Even so, it is only natural to want the exterior spaces of your home to reflect the same care and pride you put into your interiors.

What then are your options? There are attractive yard ornaments on the market, but they can be quite costly. Even do-it-yourself projects like setting up an actual Koi pond may require a substantial investment, and will still need hours of upkeep.

Painted garden art is an enjoyable and inexpensive way to give your gardens, courtyard, patio, or entryway artful touches that are attractive and surprisingly easy to do.

These pieces need little or no maintenance and will continue to enhance any outdoor area for years to come. Combining painted pieces with live flowers and plants can give even the most neglected corner new life and visual interest.

The projects in this book are designed for beginning painters and for people with little or no previous art experience. Detailed step-by-step instructions, patterns, and photos ensure that anyone can achieve satisfying results. In the course of creating your own garden art, you may come up with even more ways to display and enjoy it.

Since painting my first rock back in 1978, I have come to appreciate how perfectly suited this medium is for outdoor decorations that last even through the changing seasons. Painting on rocks and stones is simply easier to do, and less intimidating, than any other art form I can think of. Rocks are free in many places around the world, and manufactured stone and cast cement borders cost far less than conventional art materials. They are also widely available in standard sizes and shapes. It is hard to imagine an art activity that delivers more bang for the buck!

One of the goals of this book is to encourage readers to discover their artistic abilities. Starting with the easier projects is the best way to develop the basic skills and confidence needed to do the more challenging pieces. With just a bit of patience and practice, anyone can master this engaging and accessible art form.

Contents

Get Started

Rocks, Blocks, Borders, & Stones

Scalloped border stones, round stepping stones, retaining wall blocks, and flat rocks used to pave walkways, are all materials available at landscaping centers, home improvement stores, and in the gardening departments of hardware stores. Many of these same outlets also sell river rocks and pebbles for those who live in areas where such rocks can't be found naturally.

The quality of cement used in cast stone can vary, so if you have several places to shop, look for smoother pieces. These are easier to paint and more likely to last. Similarly, the tops of Anchor Windsor Stones® can vary. Choose less textured ones that make painting finer details possible.

Whether working on natural or manufactured stone, all these materials offer the exciting opportunity to create art in three dimensions. Before beginning, always wash all surfaces and allow them to dry.

Paints & Primers

A number of paint types are formulated to hold up well outdoors. DecoArt Patio Paint is always my first choice. It's a craft acrylic with a sealer built-in to help resist weathering. It comes in a wide range of colors and is usually sold in two ounce bottles.

For large pieces, exterior latex house paint may be a better choice. A pint or quart of a medium green can be lightened or darkened with Patio Paint colors.

Rather than buying dozens of colors, stick to black, white, and the primary colors, plus green, and you can combine them to make any shade you may need. Whichever paint you use, make sure it is water based and intended for outdoor use.

Because the composition of rocks and manufactured stone can vary, I recommend using a primer like latex Kilz™, which bonds with any surface and ensures that subsequent layers of paint stay put as well.

Brushes

All the projects in this book can be done with just a handful of brushes. For base coats and large areas, choose one of the inexpensive utility brushes sold in hardware and home improvement stores. They are narrow enough to dip into small paint cans, but large enough to cover rocks and stones quickly. The 1" and 3" size are most versatile.

Loew-Cornell's small 791 Filbert brush in size 6 is a perfect size for filling in colors, blending and even for outlines. The stiff white bristles hold up well and the slightly rounded edges make it an easy brush to use.

For fine lines and delicate details, Loew-Cornell's Script Liner brush in size 0 or 1 is my choice for its ability to carry a lot of paint and to hold its shape through long use.

When making Stone Planters and Blooming Borders, a small deerfoot stippler, scrubber, or stenciling brush is helpful. Loew-Cornell also makes a foam-tipped Berry Maker™ tool perfect for small, tidy dots and spots.

And that's it! There is no need to spend a lot of money on brushes when a few well-chosen ones will do.

Sealers

DecoArt Patio Paint was especially formulated for use on concrete and stone. It has a built-in sealer that resist weathering. However, even the best paints will sometimes show some wear and tear when exposed to the elements. Adding an extra coat or two of clear sealer will protect and extend the life of your outdoor art work. Krylon makes an easy-to-use spray-on sealer in both gloss and satin finish. It does not yellow and seems to perform well in a wide variety of climates.

If you prefer a brush-on sealer, consider using a marine coating ordinarily used to protect boats. These are available at larger hardware and paint stores as well as from marine specialty outlets. Marine coating is an excellent choice for sealing the Faux Fish Pond while giving the surface a realistic "wet" look.

Transferring Patterns

Duplicate the patterns provided by placing **tracing paper** over the designs and drawing over the outlines, or by scanning the pages and printing them out. Next, place **graphite paper** (for dark lines) or **transfer paper** (for light lines) between your duplicated pattern and the stone surface, or, for a template, upon heavier paper like **poster board** or **card stock**. Tape the edges to hold them in place. Retrace the outlines with a pencil, exerting firm pressure to ensure the design is fully transferred.

If making a reusable template, cut out the pattern with **scissors** and use a **utility knife** to excise small interior details like eyes. Once the main outlines are in place, use the details provided on the patterns as a guide to adding other features. Templates are especially useful if you will be making multiples of the same project.

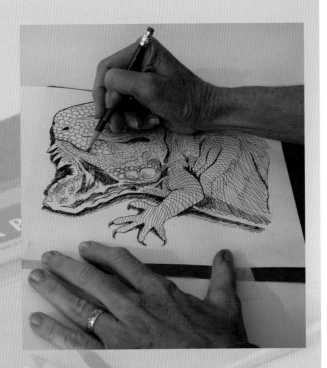

Other Supplies

White charcoal pencils are handy for sketching guidelines on dark backgrounds. **Colored pencils** can be useful for drawing on light colored backgrounds, or where regular pencil lines might show through the paint. **Recycled plastic lids** make fine palettes for mixing paint. Layers of **newspaper** can protect the painting surface while also providing a place to make test strokes and for wiping excess paint or water from brushes.

Flower and leaf stamping tools are sold at craft stores, but custom stamps can be made easily out of **styrofoam scraps** often used as packing material. Use the patterns provided to trace the shapes, then cut them out with sharp scissors or a utility knife. Leaves can be stamped on with single shapes, but for flowers, cut out a larger circle to use as the base. **Rubber cement** is ideal for attaching the petals and center to the base because it creates a flexible bond.

Painting Techniques & Tips

If you have not done much painting, it may seem mysterious, perhaps even a little scary. But water-based acrylic and latex paints are easy to use and very forgiving. Any mistake can be blotted away while wet or simply painted over once the area dries.

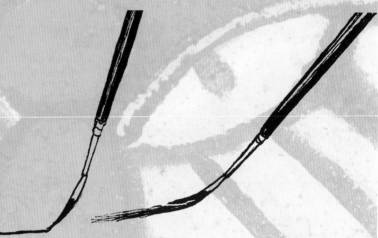

A few simple tips will help you achieve attractive results. The first is to match your brush size to the area you are painting. A brush that is too large makes it tricky to maneuver in tight places. Using a small brush can turn painting larger areas into a time-consuming chore.

Hold the brush at a more upright angle to allow the paint to flow from the tip for finer lines and more control. Stroking at a sideways angle forces the paint to come from the center of the bristles, making lines that are thicker and less precise. Always start with a damp, but not dripping, brush. Another tip is to apply paint in long, smooth strokes rather than trying to "sketch" with short, tentative strokes.

Adjust the consistency of acrylic and latex paints by adding small increments of water until the paint is loose enough to go on easily without being runny. Make test strokes until you develop a feel for how much water to add.

Creating Highlights & Shadows

Here are three basic steps to more realistic looking painting. Begin with a base coat or main color. Next, paint shadows on the lower sides of your subject's features, using a deeper shade made by darkening the base coat.

Finally, create highlights using a lighter color made by adding yellow or white to the base coat color to get a clearly contrasting shade. Together, these steps create the illusion of dimension.

Mix Custom Colors

Darken most colors by adding black. Use white to create highlights for most colors. Yellow may be substituted for making green highlights. Red may be used to darken orange, and orange or brown darkens yellow. Experiment and you will soon get a feel for color mixing.

Darken with Watery Washes

Make a transparent wash by adding enough water to any paint. Use it to tint or shade an area without obscuring underlying details.

Make Soft Highlights with a Dry Brush

Pick up paint with a dry brush and wipe off excess pigment before scrubbing the remainder on to get a softly diffused look.

Think of all the places waiting to be transformed with garden art.

Give plain steps and walls new life!

Are You Ready to Rock Your World?

Elephants on Parade

Borders define flower beds and pathways, but with the addition of a little paint, they can also be a source of drama and visual interest, even when flowers are out of season. These pigmy elephants turn plain borders into exotic accent pieces using just two colors. Measure the area where the border will go. Straight borders are two feet long and curved pieces are twenty-eight inches long. Corner pieces are also available. Layout the unpainted pieces to determine which way you want to face your parading pachyderms.

1 Make a Template and Trace the Pattern

Border stones should be clean and dry. Copy the pattern, (page 97), and transfer it onto heavy card stock or poster board to make a reusable template. Cut out the ear, eye, and tusk outlines with a small utility knife, then place the template to correspond with each scalloped shape. Use a regular graphite pencil to draw around the shape and to add the details. Repeat this process until the entire border is covered.

Supply List
- **Scalloped cement borders straight and/or curved**
- **Card stock/poster board**
- **Pencil**
- **Liner brush**
- **Size 6 filbert brush**
- **Small stiff-bristled brush**
- **DecoArt Patio Paints or exterior-quality acrylic or latex paints in:**
  Black
  White

See patterns page 98.

2 Paint the Main Outlines

Go over all the main outlines with black paint. A small filbert brush turned on its side will make clear, distinct outlines. Also outline the ear shapes.

Tip: *For smooth paint lines, always start with a damp brush*

3 Paint the Eyes, Tusks, and Wrinkles

Switch to a liner brush and loosen the paint with a bit of water, if needed, to ensure fine, unbroken lines. Outline around the tusks and paint the eyes.

Give the knees several small, curved wrinkle lines, and do the same along the front of the trunk as shown above.

4 Fill in Empty Spaces

Using solid black paint, fill in the areas between and around the legs of each elephant. When used this way, dark paint has the effect of visually "erasing" those spaces.

5 Define Separations

Along the top of the border, use black paint to separate the head of each elephant from the rear end of the elephant in front of it.

6 Paint Shadows

Make a loose wash by adding just enough water to black paint to make it transparent but not runny. Use a filbert brush to shade a wide, curved space along the underside of each elephant. Leave a narrow edge uncovered between the stomach and the black space below to ensure that the elephant's shape is well defined. Shadow below the ears and add a crease.

7 Add Soft Highlights

A small, stiff-bristled brush is ideal for creating soft highlights. Pick up white paint, then wipe off most of it so that what is left must be scrubbed into place along the sides as shown. Highlight along the top of each curved segment as well, feathering the edges and not painting over black lines.

Other areas to be highlighted in this way are the top of the head and the top of each ear.

8 Paint the Toenails

Use a clean liner brush and white paint to fill in the half-round toenail shapes at the bottom of each foot.

9 Fill in the Tusks

Fill in the small, curved tusk shapes, but leave the base of the tusks unpainted.

Why settle for boring borders when a little paint can transform them into something so special?

Use straight and curving scalloped pieces as needed. With a little modification, even angled corner pieces can be part of the parade.

To paint this corner, I simply raised the trunks and fit a baby elephant into the angle. The pattern for the baby is on page 98.

If you love frogs, try painting froggy borders. For added dimension, glue on jelly bean-sized pebbles for eyes with Liquid Nails and give them metallic gold irises. The pattern is on page 99.

Caterpillar Borders & Butterfly Walkways

Beautiful butterflies flit and flutter invitingly down a garden walkway, while serpentine edgings of multi-colored caterpillars lend definition and a touch of whimsy to the flower beds. Together, these two projects can transform any yard into a fanciful wonderland!

1 Paint Base Coat

Cover the sides, top, and ends of a curved length of scalloped tree-round edging with a bright color like Sunshine Yellow. Inexpensive utility brushes are perfect for this kind of painting. Choose a 3" brush for quick coverage, and 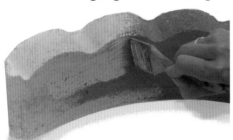 make sure to work the paint into any holes or rough places on the stone.

Caterpillar Supply List

- *Card stock or poster board for template*
- *Pencil*
- *3" utility brush*
- *Size 6 filbert brush*
- *Small, stiff-bristled brush*
- *DecoArt Patio Paint*
  (or exterior latex) paint in:
  Sunshine Yellow, Wrought Iron Black
  Tiger Lily Orange, Citrus Green
  Petunia Purple

See patterns pages 100 and 101

2 Use Templates to Transfer Design for Body & Head Segments

Trace and transfer the head and body patterns onto heavy card stock to create reusable templates. Cut out the eyes and the center marking on the body pattern. Place the head template on the first segment so that the front legs touch the bottom edge, then outline around it. Line up the body template with the curves of the other scalloped sections and draw on the design. Repeat on the other side if you plan to paint both sides. Since the head is turned to one side, add a horizontal version of two tear-drops across the top of that scallop with the pattern provided.

19

3 Paint Black Around Back Legs

Use a size 6 filbert brush to paint around the legs and along the bottom curve of the body.

4 Fill in Front Legs & Eyes

Paint around the pointy ends of the two front legs below the head segment, then fill in the eyes.

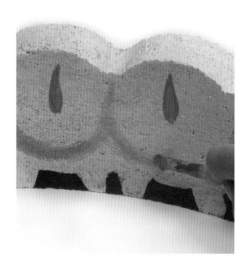

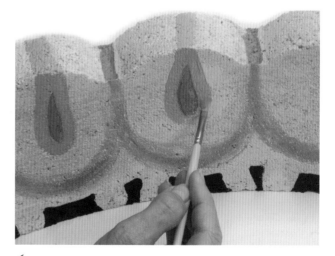

5 Paint Orange Markings

Rinse your brush and use bright orange to fill in the center of all the teardrop-shapes. Define the body segments by outlining around them. Scrubbing the paint on with a dry brush will give the lines a softer look. Use a stiff-bristled brush for best results.

6 Paint Green Markings

Return to a filbert brush and use bright green to outline around the orange centers. Extend a line of green over the top and down the other side if you are painting both sides. Outline around the orange shapes above the head as well.

7 Fill in the Face Shape

Paint the round face shape as shown. Work the paint into any holes or rough textures for consistent coverage.

8 Outline Around All Green Areas

Rinse your filbert brush before switching to purple paint to outline around all green shapes. Start at the end of your caterpillar where the paint has already dried and work up to surround the head. This outline can overlap the green layer slightly.

9 Finishing Touches to the Face

Use black or red paint to give your caterpillar a happy smile.

A foam tipped Berry Maker brush or the rubber eraser on the end of a pencil can be used to dot on a series of small round segments for the two antennae.

C-shaped gleams in the eyes will give your caterpillar more personality.

10 Add Highlights Along Top

Use a 1/2″ stiff-bristled brush to mix white and yellow to get a lighter shade. Apply it with a dry brush to the very top and over the edge onto the sides to create a softly diffused look.

Encircle a flower bed with a set of colorful caterpillars.

These cute caterpillars were made by painting sets of round river rocks.

A real caterpillar was the inspiration for this design. Use a straight piece of scalloped edging, then affix a flat, round head rock with Liquid Nails.

Butterfly Walkways

Butterfly Walkways

See patterns page 102 and 103

Butterfly Supply List

- *Card stock or poster board for pattern*
- *Pencil*
- *1/2" Utility Brush*
- *Size 6 Filbert Brush*
- *DecoArt Patio Paint (or exterior latex) in:*
  Wrought Iron Black
  Sprout Green
  Sunshine Yellow
  Pansy Purple
  Cloud White
  Tiger Lily Orange
  Patio Brick

1 Apply Design

Make a template from the pattern provided and use a pencil to draw around it on a clean, dry stepping stone.

2 Paint Outlines & Fill in Voids

Mix green and black paints to get a very deep shade. Use a size 6 filbert brush to outline the design. Switch to a 1/2" utility brush to fill in the larger areas and to cover the edges of the stone.

3 Paint Yellow Areas

Fill in the entire lower wings and a portion of the upper wings with bright yellow as shown.

4 Highlight Wings

Add enough white to the yellow paint to get a clearly lighter shade. Apply this with a dry brush to the top edges of the upper wings as well as to the tops of the three curving, oval shapes that extend downward in the upper wings. Highlight the four spot shapes as well.

5 Paint Purple Areas

Any deep, rich color will work, but I chose purple to complete my upper wing shapes.

6 Paint Purple Lines

Use your filbert brush, turned sideways, to create narrow purple lines that define wing segments. Place smaller purple spots and markings as shown.

7 Add Lighter Purple Accents

Add enough white to your purple paint to get a clearly lighter shade. Use it to create long oval segments in the purple wings. The tips of the lowest ovals may curve over the edge of the stone. Add a soft highlight to the decorative purple dots on both upper and lower wings.

8 Stroke on Orange Veins & Crescents

Switch to orange paint. Apply it with a clean filbert brush, extending three narrow lines down from the top of the lower wings on either side. Along the scalloped edges at the bottom, fit a small curved line of orange along the edge of each scallop.

9 Fill in Head & Body

Cover the three shapes that make up the head and body segments of the butterfly with a deep reddish-brown color like Patio Brick. Leave dark outlines in place around each element to define them. Any medium sized brush can be used.

10 Apply Soft Details to Body

Use a stiff brush to add white to yellow paint to get a pale color. Wipe most of the pigment off your brush before encircling each segment with a soft outline. Add a C-shaped highlight to the chest, then scrub on a series of curved bands on the abdomen below.

11 Shade Wings with Purple Wash

Add realistic shadows with a watery wash. Pick up a small amount of purple on a clean brush, then add enough water to dilute the pigment. Use it to shadow the lower edges of the yellow portions of both upper wings.

12 Paint Two Black Eyes

Use a filbert brush to place two widely-spaced black oval eyes in the head shape.

13 Add Texture to Stripes

Still using black paint, turn your filbert brush sideways and use it to create a series of short lines along the curve of each band on the abdomen to suggest a furry look.

14 Paint White Spots & Accents

Apply white spots all along the edges of the purple wings with a clean filbert brush. At the bottom of the lower yellow wings, add a curved swath of white between the purple circle and the decorative marking above it.

15 Stipple on Antennae

An easy way to make a series of dots is to pick up paint on the rounded end of a small brush and tap the paint into place. The dots get smaller as the paint runs out. If you must reload, tap more lightly to keep the dots in proportion.

16 Tidy Up the Edges

Use black paint to reinforce contrast between the edges of the butterfly and the deep green background as well as to smooth and redefine the shapes. Other wing colors and accent colors may be used, along with different wing shapes. Square stepping stone shapes add to the variety of butterfly options. Actual butterfly photos are a wonderful source of inspiration!

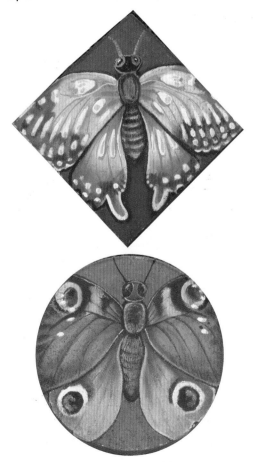

Stepping stones can be square or round, realistic or fanciful.

Stone Planter

Turn a cast stone block used for retaining walls into an elegant basket of blooms sure to beautify any spot. A grouping of several baskets can dress up a set of steps or add lasting color to a patio or courtyard.

The size and shape of the Windsor stone (above) is ideal, but other stones, both manufactured and natural, can also be transformed into flower-filled baskets. Note that there are differences in the quality of manufactured stone. Choose a stone with the least amount of texture on top. Stone colors also vary, but this will not effect the look of the finished piece unless you choose to have the color show through.

See pattern pages 104, 105, and 106

Supply List

- *Anchor Windsor ™ Stone or similarly shaped rock*
- *Ruler*
- *White charcoal pencil*
- *1" utility brush*
- *Liner brush size 0 or 1*
- *Plaid Scrubber size 4, (or Loew-Cornell Berry-Maker ™ or a short round stiff brush)*
- *Styrofoam scraps for leaf stamp*
- *Utility knife*
- *DecoArt Patio Paint in:*
    Wrought Iron Black
    Sprout Green
    Sunshine Yellow
    Tango Blue
    Cloud White

1 Layout and Base Coat

Use a ruler to mark the center of the stone about three inches from the base. Extend a slightly upward curving line to the edge on either side and wrap it around the corners and across the back. Cover the lower portion of the block with black paint, using a 1" utility brush.

2 Paint the Top

Combine Sprout Green and black to get a deep green color. Use a utility brush to cover the upper portion of the block with this color. Work paint into the texture of the top for solid coverage.

3 Lay Out Basket Weave

Draw a row of rectangles along the basket top, (A.) Lightly mark the midpoint of that line, then center a set of curved bands below it, beginning 1/2" down, (B.) Add two similar sets of bands on either side, but slightly higher, (C.) Fit one more set on either side of these, lined up with the first set, (D.) Repeat on the back. On the sides, fit three sets of bands. Place upright elements in the center of each set, (E.) Draw slanted lines along the base, (F.)

4 Paint Basket Top

Use a size 6 filbert brush and white paint to fill in the small rectangles that make up the top of the basket. Continue painting them around the sides and across the back. Leave small spaces between each segment to keep them well defined.

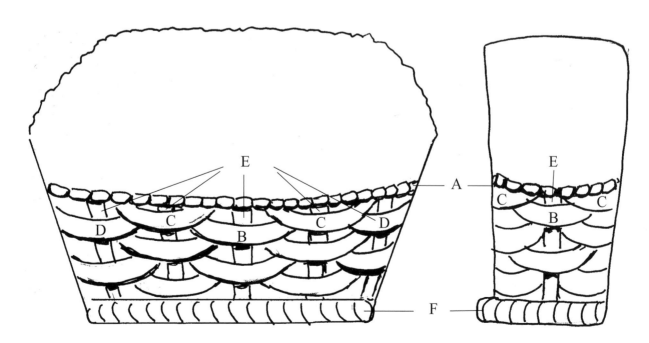

Basket weave design, front and side

5 Paint Basket Weave

Use a filbert brush and white paint to fill in the bands, keeping all edges separated. Carefully paint upright elements for the weave, fitting them between the bands. Narrow spaces between keep all elements distinct.

6 Paint Basket Base

Windsor stones have a small ledge along the bottom that enhances the design. Paint the slanting bands as shown. Use a liner brush and black paint to define these, and to touch up the weaving any place bands overlapped each other.

7 Cut Out Leaf Stamp

Use the leaf pattern provided to outline the shape, then cut it out with a utility knife. Scrap foam packing material is easy to cut and flexible enough to use as a stamp even around corners.

Leaf pattern—actual size.

Use a sharp utility knife.

8 Load Leaf Stamp

Pour out a small puddle of green paint. This color is Sprout Green but any medium green will work. Load your leaf stamp and test it on newspaper to remove excess paint before pressing firmly onto your stone.

9 Layer on Leaves

Vary the angle and placement of your leaves, and make sure some leaves overlap the sides of the basket. Bend leaves around corners and over edges to cover the top of the stone.

10 Add Lighter Leaves

Mix yellow paint into the leaf color to get a much lighter color. Sprinkle another set of leaves this color over the stone, mostly in the upper half. Make sure you bend or "see-saw" the stamp around corners to disguise the sharp edges.

11 Paint Leaf Details

Plain leaves have a stylized look. For a more realistic appearance, add creases down the centers, using a liner brush. On the darker colored leaves, use the same green-black mix used as the base coat. Also use it to separate darker green leaves that are overlapping. On the lighter leaves, paint the center vein using the original leaf color. Look for places where lighter green leaves touch or overlap and divide them. Touch up any leaf shapes that have ragged edges, and fill in any pits or gaps where coverage was incomplete.

12 Paint Shadows

Use a filbert brush and black paint loosened with water to create soft shadows below the basket where leaves overhang.

13 Sketch Bloom Shapes on Front, Back, & Sides of Stone

Allow the leaves to dry thoroughly before using a white charcoal pencil to draw on ovals 2" wide. Scatter them around, changing the angles and placing some so that they are touching or overlapping, and perching others on corners or edges. Try to put them in areas where they will fill in bare spots or where they will cover portions of several leaves rather than covering up one entire leaf.

Don't neglect the sides when sketching on bloom ovals. Try to make three full flowers plus several partial corner blossoms. A dozen or more will fit around the stone's top.

14 Undercoat Blooms

Filling in the blooms with an undercoat ensures that the flowers stand out clearly when painted. Apply black paint, softened with deep blue, using a filbert or other small brush, to fill in the ovals. Give them slightly uneven outside edges. It may take two coats for solid coverage.

Color swatch for flower undercoat

Color swatch for pale petals

Color swatch for darker tones

15 Dab on Pale Petals

Mix a tiny amount of blue into a puddle of white to get a very pale blue. Use a short and stiff, round brush, scrubber, or foam-tipped Berry-Maker, to daub irregular dots of color along the top curve of each bloom oval, leaving a narrow edge of dark undercoat uncovered to define the shape. Dot a few more light petal shapes into the center, but leave dark spaces showing.

16 Add Darker Blue Tones

Add more blue paint to the light mixture to get a deeper shade of blue. Daub it on along the lower curve of each bloom, again leaving an outline of the dark undercoat uncovered.

17 Blend & Soften Petals

Use the same darker blue to lightly blend and soften the petal colors where they meet. Be careful not to over-blend and obliterate the dark fragments of undercoat showing through, because these give the flowers more texture. The blooms do not have to be identical, and your planter will look more realistic if there is some variation among the flower heads.

Create different looks by changing the color of the blossoms, the basket, and even the leaves. I used maroon, made by mixing red and black, as the base coat for these pink flowers, with reddish-pink accents and pale pink highlights. Rather than a white basket, I used the brown Windsor stone color for the weave. Dark paint around the basket elements make them stand out, as do the lighter brown highlights. Shades of purple, lavender, orange, or yellow will all make beautiful blooms.

Below are more variations. The first is a smaller version of a Windsor-type stone. The center piece is an interlocking paver turned on one end. The third planter was painted on a natural rock shape.

Dress up a set of steps or an entry.

Plain planters can be turned into address stones or personalized with a family name.

Ever-blooming Stone Planters add an elegant touch of color anywhere.

Many variations are possible, but simple designs are best due to the rough texture of the top surface. Personalized stones make great gifts.

Fishy Flower Beds

This sunny goldfish flower bed is an easy way to add color to any outdoor space. Paint a single fish or group several together. The scalloped border sections may be combined in different ways to create a variety of fishy landscaping elements that will really make a splash. Change the colors and other details to create endless variations. Long after the growing season is over, your decorative fish will continue to serve as attractive outdoor accents.

1 Lay Out Scalloped Border Pieces

Use a picnic table or make a work space using saw horses and a piece of rigid plywood. Cover the surface with newspaper or newsprint. Make sure your border pieces are clean and dry.

Supply List

- *A selection of scalloped border pieces including:*
    - *Two curved tree rounds*
    - *Two corner pieces*
- *Red colored pencil*
- *2"-3" utility brush*
- *1/2" or 1" utility brush*
- *Filbert brush, size 6*
- *Exterior Quality Latex Paint in:*
    - *Bright Yellow*
    - *Bright Red*
- *DecoArt Patio Paint in Cloud White Wrought Iron Black*

2 Paint Under Coat

A light base coat will help subsequent colors pop. Use a wide, slightly dampened brush to cover all the top, outer sides, and at least the upper half of the inner sides. Also paint the ends of each section. Let dry.

3 Paint Base Coat

Mix a half cup of yellow paint with an equal amount of bright red to get orange. Rinse your brush before covering all the yellow paint, including all ends.

4 Create Highlights

Switch to a one inch wide brush and use yellow paint to create highlights on the top and sides of the scallops.

5 Add Shadows

Rinse and dry your brush then add a red shadow to the bottom of the fish body all the way around. A dry brush allows you to scrub the paint on for a blended look. Do not shadow the tail.

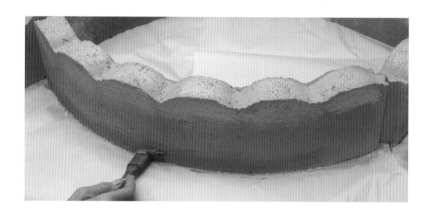

6 Sketch on Design

Use a red colored pencil to draw a fin, starting in the center of the first scallop and ending in the middle of the second one. Add C-shaped scales. On the head, draw an eye below the first full scallop, and add a curving mouth and a gill line. Do the same on the other side of the fish shape. Use the pattern as a guide.

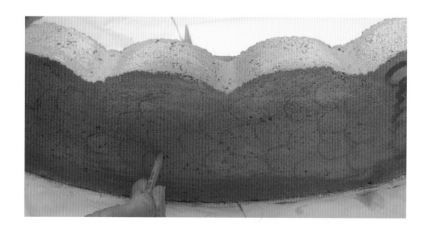

Fishy flower bed pattern

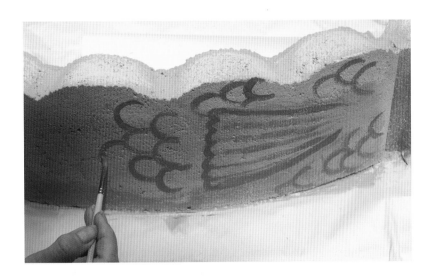

7 Paint Fin and Scales

Use a filbert brush and red paint to go over all your sketched-on guidelines. Add narrow lines to the insides of the side fins. Leave spaces here and there among the scales for a random look. If needed, add a small amount of water to the paint to ensure smooth, clean lines.

8 Paint Eyes and Mouth

Paint the mouth line in one smooth stroke. Fill in the eye with solid red. You can be creative and give your fish different features if you'd like.

9 Paint Red Tail Lines

Add a series of graceful, flowing lines to either side of both tail fins. Extend the lines all the way around the notched ends of the stone.

10 Darken Base of Tail

Use the same red paint on a dry brush to softly darken the base of the tail where it joins the fish body. Do this to both sides of each tail fin.

11 Paint Yellow Tail Lines

Switch to yellow paint to add wavy lines between the red ones, giving the tail more color and detail.

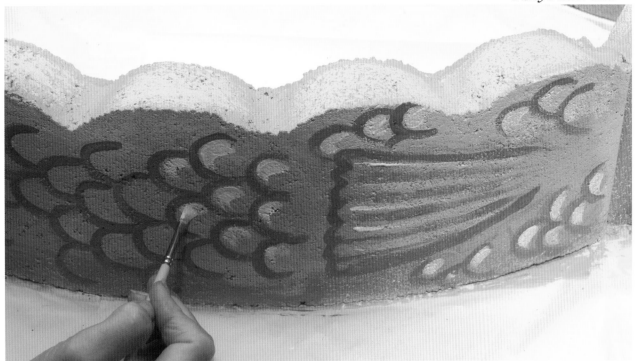

12 Add Yellow Touches to the Body

Simple crescent-shaped strokes of yellow placed in the upper half of each scale, along with yellow lines set between the red ones on the fins, are easy details that add loads of visual interest.

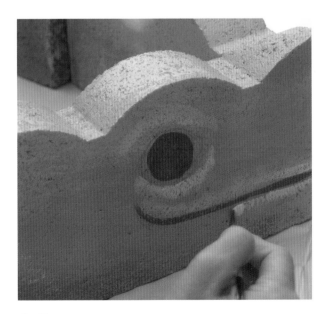

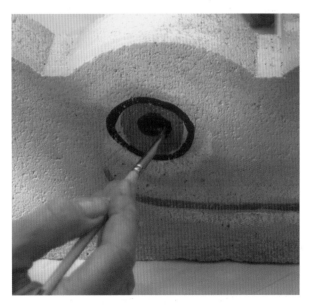

13 Paint Yellow Accents on Face

Use a dry brush to add soft highlights above and below the eye as shown, then add more soft outlines above and below the mouth on both sides.

14 Paint the Eyes

Encircle the eyes with an outline of solid black paint. Place a round black pupil in the center.

15 Give the Eyes their "Sparkle"

Place two round dots of white paint in the upper eye where the pupil and iris meet and suddenly your fish will appear to be looking back at you. The completed fish can now be filled with flowers. If you prefer to display your fish as garden ornament, paint the inside walls completely for a more finished look.

More "Fishy" Shapes to Paint

The same basic border pieces can make a variety of fish-shaped beds in sizes ranging from small to extra large. Imagine a colorful school of fish in your yard!

Two corner pieces and two straight pieces.

Four corner pieces.

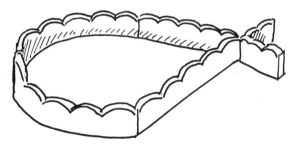

Two tree rounds, two straight pieces, and one corner piece.

Two curved tree round pieces and one corner piece.

Four straight borders and one corner piece.

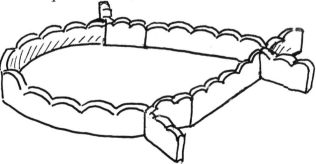

Two tree rounds, two straight pieces, and three corner pieces.

42

More Ideas

Sunny yellow mums, along with a sprinkling of several varieties of purple flowers, make for a lush late-season display. Petunias, marigolds and other low-growing flowering plants make it easy to turn your Fishy Flower Bed into a focal point.

This variation is made by combining two tree rounds with a corner piece for the tail. It is slightly smaller, with a seam in the center of the face where the sections meet, so make sure your mouth line extends into both the notch and the V-shaped ends to minimize the joint. I filled this fish with cheerful dwarf zinnias.

Shades of blue and green formed the base coat for this fish, with increased amounts of white blended into the lower half of the blue body. Yellow lines in a diagonal cross-hatch create a simple suggestion of scales. If you have the room, consider creating a whole school of these whimsical, flower-filled art pieces.

Petaled Pathways

Bold and beautiful Hardy Hibiscus blossoms were my inspiration for a set of stepping stones to enhance any pathway. I chose soft pastels but they can also be painted in hot colors like orange, red, and yellow for a more tropical effect. One word of caution; red pigments tend to be less stable, and may fade in bright sunshine. Retouching is easy and will keep them looking bright.

Supply List
- *12" round cast stepping stone.*
- *Pencil*
- *1" utility brush*
- *Size 6 filbert brush*
- *DecoArt Patio Paint in*
  Wrought Iron Black
  Sprout Green
  Petunia Purple
  Cloud White
  Geranium Red
  Sunshine Yellow

1 Draw Center Star

Use a pencil to sketch a standard, five-pointed star in the center of the stepping stone.

2 Define Petal Shapes

Extend lines out from each point, rounding the corners to form the petals. Give each petal's outer edge a slightly different shape as shown above.

45

3 Paint Edges & Outlines

Darken green paint with enough black to make a deep shade. Use a 1" brush to paint around the petal edges and at least halfway down the sides. Switch to a small brush to fill in the points of the center star, and to paint the lines that divide the petals.

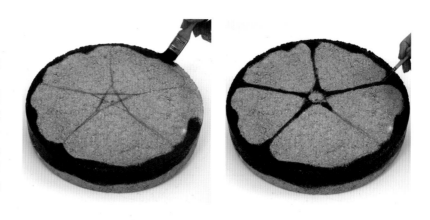

4 Fill in the Petal Shapes

Rinse out the 1" brush and use it to paint the petals. I chose Petunia Purple but other colors may be used. The swatch below shows how to mix black and white with almost any base color to create the shades needed for shadowing and highlighting.

5 Add Shadowing

Mix just enough black into your petal color to get a much darker shade. Use your 1" brush to give the upper half of each petal one or two large shadows, depending on whether the petal has one indent along the outside edge, or two. Avoid covering up the outside edges of the petals. Turn the brush sideways to give the innermost edges of the shadows some streaky lines pointing toward the flower center.

6 Highlight the Petals

Switch to a 1/2" brush and use it to mix white into your petal color to get a very pale shade. Apply this color narrowly along the very outside edges of the petals all the way around, then turn the brush sideways and add a few streaks outward from the center, allowing them to overlap into the shadowed areas here and there.

7 Paint the Center

Use a filbert brush to dab red paint into the flower's center, then create narrow lines that radiate outward from the center corner of each petal. Make some shorter and some longer for a more natural look.

8 Soften Contrasts

Now that all the main colors are in place, use the side of 1" brush and your original petal color to blend and soften the midsection of each petal by stroking some lines outward into the shadowed areas. This is a subtle step so don't overdo it. Two or three soft, narrow lines into the edges of the shadows are enough.

9 Stipple Pollen Dots into Center

Use a bright yellow color to give the center of the flower a bit of eye-catching detail. An easy way to stipple is to turn a small brush around and use the tip of the handle to pick up paint, then tap it into place. The first tap or two will be larger, but add several more smaller taps to make a variety of sizes.

Create an instant pathway by setting a row of stones into grass. Over time they will work their way down and set into the soil.

Any simple flower design will translate nicely onto a stepping stone. Layers of sunny yellow petals are shadowed with reddish-brown near a solid, dark brown center. The petals are outlined in dark brown and then highlighted with paler yellow. Reddish-brown dots highlight the center.

Pea-sized gravel makes a low-maintenance back-drop for painted stepping stones.

Turned on its side, this stepping stone became the canvas for a floral accent rock.

Colored mulch gives the stones a different look. A combination of flowers and butterflies beckons visitors to explore your garden.

Blooming Borders

Fill your garden with bright, beautiful, flowering borders. In far less time than it would take to prepare the ground, plant, water, grow, and weed real flowers, you can have a set of gorgeous stone borders whose flowers and leaves are stamped on. With so many options for flower types, leaf shapes and color combinations, your Blooming Borders can be uniquely individualized. Display them alone or to supplement actual flower beds.

1 Paint the Base Coat

Mix black and green paint to get a very dark green shade and use a wide utility brush to cover top, sides, and ends of each border piece. Work the paint in for complete coverage.

Supply List
- *Scalloped borders, curved or straight*
- *1/2" thick Styrofoam sheet, utility knife and rubber cement (or buy commercial flower and leaf stamps)*
- *2"-3" utility brush*
- *Liner brush, size 0 or 1*
- *DecoArt Patio Paint in:*
  Sprout Green, Wrought Iron Black
  Sunshine Yellow, Citrus Green
  Geranium Red, and Cloud White

2 Make or Buy Flower & Leaf Stamps

Check craft supply stores for foam backed flower and leaf stamps, or make your own using 1/2" thick styrofoam sheets often used as packing material. Sketch on simple flower petal and leaf shapes, and cut them out with a sharp utility knife. Cut a larger, round piece as a backing for the petals. Apply rubber cement to both surfaces and press the petals into place. Let dry for 30 minutes or more. Leaf shapes do not need a backing. Thin household sponges or colored craft foam may also be cut into shapes. See leaf and flower patterns on page 101.

3 Stamp On Lower Leaves

Sprout Green shows up nicely against the dark base coat, or use other medium green shades. Cluster these leaves along the lower half of the stone, including the ends. Paint the backside if it will be visible where you plan to display it.

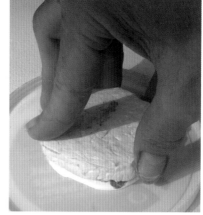

4 Stamp On Lighter Leaves

Switch to Citrus Green, or add Sunshine Yellow to your medium green shade to get a clearly lighter color. Layer these leaves on over the lower leaves and along the top. Bend some leaves around edges.

5 Pour Paint & Load Stamp

Pour out a circular puddle of paint. I mixed red and white together to get pink. Surround that puddle with a narrow circle of white paint. This will give the petals a variegated look. Press the stamp into the paint and do test stamps on newspaper to remove excess paint.

6 Apply Stamp to Stone

Place flowers randomly among the leaves both on top and down the sides. Nestle some flowers together so that petals touch or overlap while others are alone. Press firmly to ensure all petals transfer their paint, and reload as needed. Turn the stamp as you work so that the angle of the individual blossoms vary. Stamp over flowers that look faint, or have gaps in their paint, or go back later with a brush and fill them in by hand.

7 Change Flower Color, Shape or Size

Treat each scalloped section as a separate plant, changing the blossom color as you work down the border. This salmon color was made by adding yellow to the pink previously mixed. A smaller homemade stamp was used to apply the white flowers. In the example above, there are several dark gaps between the flowers and leaves. These can be filled in with partial leaves, or with an overlapping flower. Apply flowers to corners and edges by "rocking" the stamp back and forth between the two surfaces.

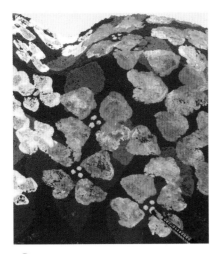

8 Add Tiny Centers

Use the tip of a liner brush handle and Sunshine Yellow paint to tap three small dots into the center of each larger flower. A single dot was added to the smaller white flowers.

9 Change the Leaves

Different sizes, shapes, and colors will create completely different looks. These heart-shaped leaves are edged in white for a dramatic effect.

10 Change the Flowers

Although stamped in the same pink/white combination, these flowers were done with a commercial stamp and have their own distinctive look.

11 More Flower Choices

Place a drop of yellow in the middle of a white circle to make these easy daisies.

12 Tidying & Touch-Ups

Use a liner brush and dark green paint to separate flowers, smooth out ragged edges, and even to underline the yellow centers to help them stand out.

Rocky the Tortoise

Combine smaller rocks with a large domed "shell" rock to create a sturdy tortoise that will make an adorable accent for your garden or water feature. The legs and head may be secured to the shell with glue, but leaving them separate allows you to pose your tortoise. Rocky can be created in virtually any size from tiny to huge. A number of variations are possible by changing colors and details. If you price the cast stone turtles sold at garden centers, you will appreciate this do-it-yourself version even more!

Choose rocks similar in shape and proportion to these. Scrub them with detergent or one of the popular bathroom cleaning products.

Supply List

- *Smooth river rocks and pebbles for the shell and body parts*
- *White charcoal pencil*
- *Regular graphite pencil*
- *Assorted brushes including: small and medium stiff bristle flats or filbert brushes*
- *Liner brush size 0 or 1*
- *DecoArt Patio Paint in Woodland Brown (or Patio Brick)*
  Sunshine or Sunflower Yellow
  Patio Brick
  Cloud White
  Wrought Iron Black

1 Select & Base Coat Body Parts

Make sure all the rocks are completely dry before covering them with the same color, usually a shade of brown or green. Use a stiff-bristled brush to paint the top sides, let dry, then turn and paint the bottoms. These were painted with Woodland Brown lightened with Sunshine Yellow. Patio Brick combined with Sunflower Yellow is also good.

2 Draw Details on Head, Feet & Tail

Once the base coat is dry, use a white char-coal pencil to sketch on the simple features. Divide the length of the head rock into a neck section and the face, and draw wide-spaced eyes. Use the pattern below as a guide to drawing toes and scales on the feet and the tail.

3 Paint Over Guidelines

Use a damp liner brush and black paint to cover the guidelines. The paint will go on more smoothly if loosened slightly with a bit of water. Remaining traces of the white guidelines can be wiped away later.

4 Create Neck Textures

Fill in those long, narrow V-shaped crease lines along the neck with a slightly different shade of brown like Patio Brick. Once that color dries, use a liner and black paint to encircle the neck with narrow, wavering and broken strokes that suggest wrinkles.

Patterns for Head, Feet, Tail, & Shell

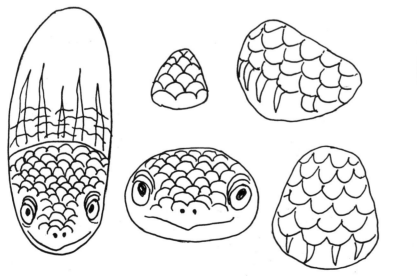

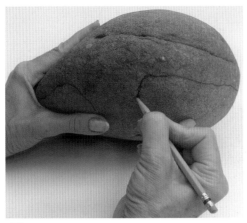

5 Draw Shell Design

Use a regular pencil to draw the edge of the shell and the side sections connecting top and bottom. Consult the patterns provided for guidance.

6 Paint Upper & Lower Shell

Mix a light beige by combining white paint with a touch of brown. Use it to cover the top and side sections of the shell. Switch to black paint to "erase" the lower portion of the tortoise in both front and back, using a medium-sized stiff brush. Let dry.

7 Draw Shell Segment Design

Make a circle at the top and divide it in two with a line that points to the center of the shell front. Cross it with a line that goes all the way down either side. Center a large shell segment in the front, and a smaller segment right above it, then fill the remaining front half of the shell with two similar sets of segments. Do the same in the back half, to end up with three levels of graduated segments. Widen the joints between all the segments so that they are double lines as shown.

8 Paint Border & Outline Segments

Use a filbert brush turned sideways to outline around each segment. Paint a series of small, solid rectangles in the border around the shell, with the first one centered below the front segment.

Define the lower edge of the shell by painting a narrow line just below the line of small rectangles.

9 Paint Segment Centers & Eyes

Fill in the center of each shell segment with a bright yellow splotch, using a stiff brush. Switch to a smaller brush to fill in the eyes with the same yellow.

10 Blend in Brown Shades

Mix yellow and brown to get a lighter brown and use a filbert brush to fill in the areas between the yellow centers and dark outlines. Wipe off the brush and use it to blend and soften.

11 Fill in Border Centers

Once all the shell segments are filled in, use the same golden brown to give each border segment a lighter center.

12 Brighten & Even Out Joints

Switch to a liner brush and white paint to add narrow white lines along the center of the joints between the shell segments. Also look for places where the joints are too narrow, or where the edges could be smoother, and fix them.

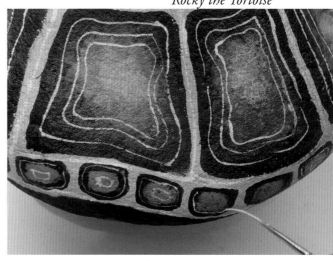

13 Add Texture Lines to Shell Segments

Use the tip of a moist liner brush and beige paint to give each shell segment a set of three very delicate, ridge-like lines concentrated in the darker outside area of the segments. Loosen the paint as needed to help it flow smoothly off the brush tip.

Once the large segments are detailed, move to the smaller border segments and give each one a tiny square in the center and another outline just inside the outer edges.

14 Finishing Touches for the Face

Use a damp paper towel to pat away any remaining white charcoal guidelines. Give each eye a black pupil that hangs from the top of the eye. Mix a tiny amount of the yellow-brown blend used as the base coat for the head. Add a touch of white to lighten it, and use a liner brush to give the tortoise lighter lids above the eyes, to outline above and below the mouth, and to highlight above the nostrils.

Add two tiny spots of white paint to each eye. An easy way to apply them is to pick up the paint with the tip of a liner brush handle and then tap or press the handle lightly against the eye.

15 Paint the Toenails

Finish the toes on all four feet by filling in the black outline of each toenail with white paint.

16 Put Rocky Together

Arrange the feet, tail, and head so that the shell rests evenly upon them. It may take some adjustment to seat the shell firmly. If you want to glue the pieces, carefully lift the shell and place a pea-sized amount of Liquid Nails™ Original Formula on each piece, then settle the shell back in place and let the glue set up, undisturbed, for at least an hour. Or keep the individual elements loose and set up your tortoise where you want to display him!

Paint a green version to display alone or with a friend.

Rocky looks right at home in a natural setting... or enjoy him as an ornament among your flower beds.

More Ideas

Here are a few more of the many ways to paint tortoises and turtles. The one on the left was put together with smooth pebbles and glue. Wood filler hides the joints. The example on the right was painted on a round stone. Instructions for this turtle can be found in my book, **The Art of Painting Animals on Rocks** (North Light Books, 1994.)

When creating a more realistic tortoise, it is helpful to have good photographs of your subject. This tortoise was made on a single rock.

To paint it, begin by drawing on the shell shape and adding the head and tucked-in feet. Use black to suggest depth around the head and legs, and mix a very deep brown to outline around the shell segments and along the border surrounding the shell. A lighter brown was used to fill in the lower portions of the shell segments. Darker brown filled in the upper half of each segment, and yellow paint, toned down with a touch of warm brown, was used to add the markings. Reddish-brown tints soften the edges of the markings, and delicate beige lines encircle the shell segments as they do on Rocky the Tortoise. The head is defined by using pale gray paint to highlight the top edge and to suggest the bumpy texture of scales across the top of the head. Use beige darkened with a touch of gray to paint the lower portions of the head. Suggest wrinkles around the neck with black paint. The legs were painted in golden yellow and then black paint was used to define the scale pattern.

Garden Gator

At more than six feet long, this life-size alligator is guaranteed to stop visitors in their tracks wherever he is displayed. The center portion makes a great flower bed. He could also be planted with prickly green succulents or cacti, or, by simply shoving the sides together, give your gator a "lean, hungry look" as he basks on the shore of a pond or along a creek bank. However you choose to display him, he is sure to attract plenty of attention!

Supply List
- *1 curbstone* • *4 straight scalloped border pieces*
- *1 curved scalloped tree ring* • *2 small oval rocks for eyes*
- *4 round or oval stones for feet, 4-6" or two square and two rectangular Pavestone Patio Pavers®*
- *Yellow colored pencil* • *Regular graphite pencil*
- *3" Utility brush* • *Size 6 filbert brush* • *Assorted small and medium stiff bristled brushes,* • *Liner brush size 1*
- *Exterior quality latex paint in: Bright green, black, bright yellow, and white*

1 Put Your Gator Together

To make a Garden Gator, assemble all the parts. A picnic table makes a handy outdoor studio. Cover the surface with newspaper to protect it. Decide which way you want the tail to curve before painting it. The curbstone for the gator above is a different color, but since it will be covered with paint, it doesn't matter.

2 Paint the Head & Body Sections

Your gator can be any color, but I used a bright, primary green with enough black paint added to darken it to a deep shade. Use a damp, 3" utility brush to cover all visible surfaces of the head and body, but don't paint the feet yet. Work the paint into any pits or rough areas. Make sure all the ends are also covered.

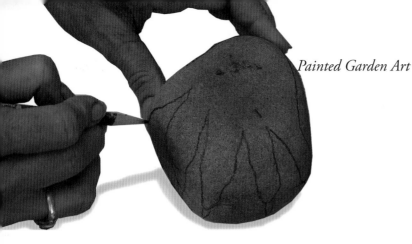

3 Draw on the Design—Feet & Body

Palm-sized, slightly angular rocks make great front feet, while rear feet may be more oval in shape. Substitute square and rectangular Pavestone Plaza Pavers™ if no natural rocks are available. Use the pattern on page 107 to help apply the feet designs to your rocks or pavers.

For the body, use a yellow colored pencil to sketch out the gator's basic elements. The pattern below will help you position the front and back legs so that they correspond to the scallops above them. There should be four body stones, two for each side. Make sure you change the direction of the front and rear legs so that both sets will match up properly, with the elbow and knee angles facing toward each other.

Paint the fingers and toes solid green.

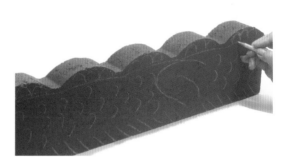

There will be a second set of front/back segments that face in the other direction.

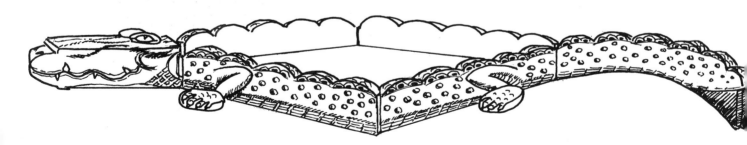

Garden Gator pattern

Draw a curving line on both sides of the tail. When painted black, the space seems to vanish.

Use Liquid Nails Original Formula in the "small projects" tube to attach the eye rocks.

4 Draw on the Design —Head & Tail

Create the illusion of a tapering tail by curving a line upward at one end. When the lower angle is painted black, it has the effect of being "erased."

On the head, draw wavy lines that suggest contours along the top. Add nostrils and a straight mouth line across the front that follows a jagged upward course on each side to end in a smile just below either eye. The ideal eye rocks are ovals several inches long with one flat side. If rocks are not available naturally in your area, small, smooth stones like these should be available at a landscaping center.

5 Paint Highlights on the Head

Pour a quarter of a cup of the original base coat color into a mixing container and set the rest aside. Mix in bright yellow to get a lighter shade perfect for creating highlights on your gator. Use a filbert brush to paint on curved eyelids, then stroke on highlights as shown, including a jaw-line parallel with the bottom of the stone. Use the pattern on page 68 for help with placing highlights.

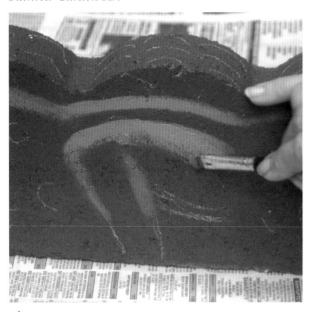

6 Paint Highlights on Legs & Back

Highlights add the illusion of dimension to the legs and define the shape of the back. Use a large, stiff-bristled brush to extend a gently curving line below the scallops, corresponding to the curving shapes above. Outline the edges of the front and back legs, then widen the highlights along the upper edges as shown.

7 Paint Highlights for Scale Texture

Fit three small crescents into each scallop, then add three or four more rows of unattached curved lines across the top of the rock, matching the ones below. Texture the gator's sides with scales by painting half-round strokes, curved-side up. Extend a few scales around the corner onto the ends as well.

8 Continue Scale Texture to End of Tail

Use light green paint to define the tapering bottom edge of the tail. Extend the same gently waving spine line along the top, but toward the tip of the tail raise the line until it ends at the top corner of the stone. The crescent-shaped ridges along the top should get smaller toward the tail tip until they are tiny at the end. Continue the patterns of scale shapes, also making them smaller near the tail tip.

9 Add Shadows & Dark Details to Front Body Sections

Mix small increments of black paint into the original green base coat color. When the color is deep enough for clear contrast, use a clean filbert brush to outline around the two front legs outside the highlights. Fill in the centers of the top ridges, and paint upside-down crescents underneath every highlighted scale. Fill in the angled crook of each leg, then moisten the paint and add shadows to the lower and outer edges of the front legs.

10 Add Shadows to the Rear Body Sections

Keep your brush damp as you apply shadows to the lower edge of each stone section. Also use this darker color to create a shadow below the curved angle of the back legs. Add more water to create a loose wash and use this to shadow along the lower edges of the folded rear legs.

11 Add Shadows to Both Sides of the Tail Section

When shadowing the bottom edge of the tail, leave the narrow line of the lighter green uncovered to help separate the tail tip from the background. Shadows and highlights work together to complete the illusion of dimension.

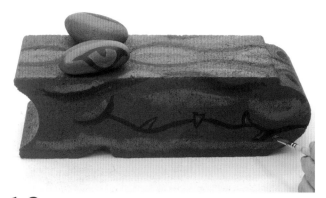

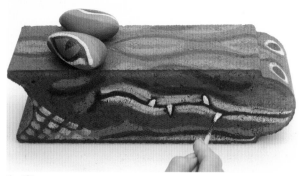

12 Paint Dark Details on Face

Use the same darkened green to create soft shadows down the center of the gator's face, to underline the highlights below the eyes, and also along the sides of the head. Switch to black paint to outline the eyes, to cover the mouth lines, and to fill in the two nostrils. Outline pointy little teeth as shown.

13 Paint Light Details on Face

Apply white paint with a clean filbert brush. Paint white outlines just outside the black lines for the eyes, and encircle the nostrils. Use a dry brush to create soft lines of white above and below the mouth. At the neck, use the width of the brush to create several diagonal rows of small, squarish scales that fit into the corner of the rock shape on each side. Finally, use full strength white paint to fill in each tooth, leaving narrow outlines of black in place to help them stand out.

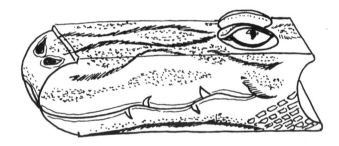

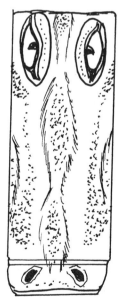

Patterns for face details—stipples indicate highlights

14 Paint Gleams in the Eyes

It is amazing how just the suggestion of light sparkling in the eyes seems to make a stone creature come to life! Use a liner brush to add two short lines, one on either side of, and slightly overlapping, the edges of the pupil.

Stagger the scales so that the sets angle slightly.

Note how scales follow the curve of the back leg.

15 Paint White Scales Lines

Paint long, narrow scales in sets of three along the bottom edge of the body. Stagger the sets slightly at a backward angle, and keep the highest one just beneath the edge of the shadowing to maintain contrast so each scale will stand out. While the size and number of sets may vary, three to four sets should fit below each corresponding scalloped shape of the stone. If the scales touch or overlap one another, go back with a liner brush and dark paint and separate them.

The scales along the rear sections are identical to the front sections, with the exception of the rear legs. There, make a row of scale lines that angle upward, curving along the inside of the folded leg and getting shorter until they stop at the inside crook.

Scales get smaller near the tail tip.

Paint around the corners so no unfinished stone shows.

On the tail section, continue the sets of scale lines, but make them shorter and thinner as they follow the curve of the tail to its tip. At the other end, paint scale lines around the stone's edges. If there are any gaps when the gator is put together, painted joints will make them less obvious.

Scale details for front feet.

Scale details for rear feet.

16 Details for the Front & Back Feet

Outline the shapes of the feet and toes with black paint and add a pointy toenail to each toe. Give the feet a scaly look to match the rest of the gator, using light green to paint curved lines along each toe that evolve into small round scales on the top. Add a line of shadow to each highlighted curve and spot as shown above. Finally, switch to white paint and add a curve of white to the top of each nail.

Give your gator a quick manicure.

17 Put the Gator Together

The width of the gator can be adjusted by changing the angle of the body segments. Place the feet so that they line up with the ends of the legs. When set up on the ground, try to level the surface so that the segment joints line up evenly. Placing the gator on gravel or mulch will make maintenance much simpler.

Prickly plants like succulents or cacti look great tucked into a Garden Gator. This fellow was painted in a simple and more stylized way that would make it an easy project for children.

Mums fill this gator with bright autumn color. Begonias, marigolds, and other annuals can also be used.

For a strictly ornamental look, leave your gator empty, with the sections pushed together. He would love to lounge by a water feature or bask by your doorstep.

71

Faux Fish Pond

Enjoy the elegant look of a koi pond without any of the maintenance and upkeep that an actual fish pond requires. Faux Fish Ponds allow you to create natural looking water features that need no plumbing, so you can set one up anywhere you'd like to create a peaceful and surprisingly realistic display.

Supply List
- *Large flat rock*
- *1" Utility brush • Card stock or poster board*
- *Size 6 Filbert Brush • White charcoal pencil*
- *Size 0 or 1 Liner Brush*
- *Kilz primer in oil based formula*
- *DecoArt Patio Paint in:*
  Wrought Iron Black
  Sprout Green
  Sunshine Yellow
  Citrus Green
  Tiger Lily Orange
  Geranium Red
  Patio Brick, Cloud White
- *Krylon or other exterior clear sealer in high gloss*

See patterns pages 108 and 109

Tip: *When using man-made stones, priming with oil based Kilz should help avoid problems with peeling or blistering.*

1 Choose a Stone

The upper example is a Pavestone® Sandstone System™, a type of manufactured stone available at most garden supply and home improvement stores. These stones come in several shapes and sizes. The lower example is a natural field stone. Any flat stone can be turned into a fish pond.

2 Paint the Sides & Outer Edges

Apply a coat of Kilz brand primer to top and sides first to ensure that subsequent paint layers will last. Let dry.
Use a 1" utility brush and a mixture of black, softened with green paint, to create very dark sides. Work your way several inches into the rock's top, encircling the stone with this color.

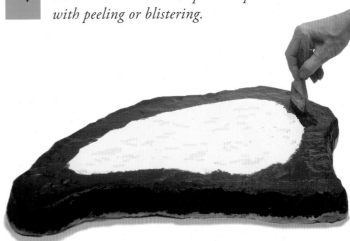

73

3 Add & Blend Lighter Green Shades

Without rinsing your brush, begin picking up a lighter shade of green and blending it into the edges of darker paint, continuing to work in circles toward the center of the stone.

4 Dapple the Center

Mix a slightly lighter shade of green by adding yellow. Use a clean brush to dab and blend this lighter color into the center. Let dry.

5 Create Dark Textures

Use a filbert brush and dark green paint to make random, squiggly lines that create the illusion of crevices and crannies at the bottom of the pond.

6 Transfer Patterns

Trace the patterns provided for fish and lily pads onto stiff card stock. Arrange them as you wish on the stone, then use a sharp white charcoal pencil to outline around them.

7 Undercoat Fish & Lilies

Bright yellow paint helps subsequent colors stand out clearly from the background. Give the mostly white fish one coat. The orange fish each need two coats. The lily pads also need two coats. Stroking outward from the center of each leaf helps establish the underlying structure that may show through to enhance the finished leaves.

8 Add Shadows

Dark shadows below each element reinforce the illusion that they have dimension and also help them stand out. Use a liner brush and the same deep green that surrounds the pond edges to outline and separate any overlapping elements.

9 Paint the Lily Pads

Apply Citrus Green or similar lime green shade, and use it to cover each lily pad. Stroke outward from the center with a filbert brush. Leave a narrow line of yellow showing around the edges.

10 Paint the Ribs of the Lily Pads

For a more natural look, use Sprout Green applied with a dry brush to create 8-9 narrow, slightly diffused-looking ribs. Switch to a liner brush and loosen darker green paint to add a very narrow line down the center of each rib.

11 Add Texture to Fins

Rinse your liner brush and switch to black paint softened with a touch of orange. Create a fringe of tiny strokes to detail the fins as shown.

12 Fill in Largest Fish

Use Tiger Lily Orange paint to fill in the lower side of the fish, as well as fanning strokes of orange out along the tops and sides of the fins. (See color swatch A.)

13 Paint Reddish Details

Add Geranium Red or other bright red color to your orange paint to get a clearly deeper shade, (Swatch B.) Use it to suggest the contours of the fish, the gill line, and an oval around the eye, as well as along the base of the top fin and along the lower body toward the tail.

14 Add Darker Touches

Darken your red mixture with a trace of black to get a deeper color, (Swatch C.) Use it to shade the head below the eye, the line of the top fin, and to darken the lower center of the fish to the tail fin. Leave a line of lighter paint uncovered along the fish's bottom edge.

15 Paint Dark Details

Darken the rusty red to get a deeper shade by adding a bit more black, (Swatch D.) With a damp liner brush, add delicate lines to the fins at the sides and top. Darken the gill line and encircle the eye. Loosen the paint slightly with water before adding curved cross-hatching to suggest scales.

16 Paint Light Details

Rinse your liner before mixing white with a touch of yellow to get a creamy color, (Swatch E.) Lighten the edges and ends of the three body fins showing.

Tip: *Place a square of clear plastic over swatches below and dab on paint samples to check for color matches.*

A. Orange B. Orange + Red

C. Orange + Red + Black D. Swatch C + more Black

E. White + Yellow F. Swatch E + Orange

17 Create Subtle Highlights

Add a trace of orange to the creamy color and use a filbert brush to apply a wedge of this pastel shade to the head as shown, (Swatch F.)

Goldfish Color Swatches

18 Fill in Smallest Fish

Use a mix of orange and red to create a deep orange shade. Fill in the entire shape of the fish with this color, leaving only a very narrow line of the yellow base coat showing along the edges.

19 Paint Highlights

Yellow paint, warmed with a bit of orange, will help define a spine line. Apply with a liner, or use a filbert brush turned sideways. Along the bottom edge of the body, paint two small, rounded fin shapes.

20 Add Shadows

Switch back to the rusty red used to shade the largest fish. Add a line of soft shadow along the lower edge of the fish, and a very narrow shadow along the highlighted top fin.

21 Paint White Areas

Fill in the third fish with solid white paint. Leave the spotted portions uncovered or just paint the spots on top of the white layer.

22 Paint Deep Orange Spots

Use the same red-orange shade used for the smallest fish to paint the markings on the white fish. Dab the smaller spots on with a liner or the tip of a filbert brush.

23 Add Black Markings

Add visual interest by making the black markings look delicate or stippled in contrast to the more solid looking orange spots. Allow them to overlap the larger orange areas as shown. Goldfish and koi come in a wide variety of color combinations. Color photos of actual fish may inspire you to try painting different kinds.

24 Paint Gray Shadows

Combine white and black to get a medium gray color. Use it to add a shadow along the underside of the white fish's head. Shadow beneath the larger fish's head where it overlaps the white fish's back. Also use gray to stroke narrow lines outward along the fins.

25 Paint Black Eyes

With a liner brush, fill in the black eye that shows on each fish. Keep the eyes small for a more realistic look. I added a lighter orange highlight to the orange marking on the white fish's head, too.

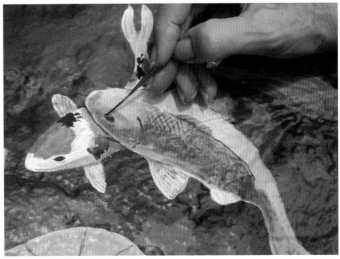

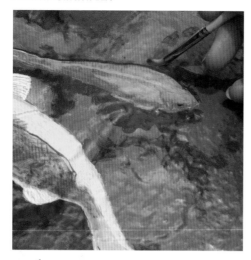

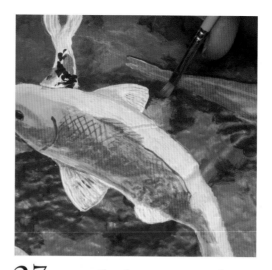

26 Redefine with Outlines

Once the fish are finished, narrow outlines of dark green will ensure that they stand out clearly.

27 Use Shadows to Heighten Contrast

Because the shadows in the water were painted randomly, some areas may need refining. The fin shape on the biggest fish here is too similar to the mottled water surrounding it. Changing the shape of the shadows helps the fin stand out. Look for areas that could use similar definition.

28 Final Touches

Add water to a small amount of reddish-brown to make a watery wash, and use a filbert brush to tint the very edges of each water lily leaf, and to stroke soft tints outward from the center of each leaf. Look for areas that need touching up or that seem unfinished, and add contrast or clearer outlines to define them. There are several products that will give your pond a shiny finish. Krylon makes a spray-on finish in gloss that holds up well outdoors. Another option is to brush on a clear marine coating used to coat boat hulls. Sealers add protection and add to the illusion of actual water in the pond. Watch for dullness and re-seal as needed. Sealing the bottom and sides of the rock further protects your artwork.

Ideas for Customizing Your Pond

The textured surface of manufactured stones resembles rippled water when painted and sealed with a glossy finish. Use several layers of flat stones to surround your faux fish pond, allowing the top layer to slightly overlap the edges for a more realistic appearance.

A small round stone can be painted to look like a water lily. Place it near the lily pads to enhance the illusion that the pond is real.

*The turtle is a variation of the tortoise project in this book. Step-by-step instructions for painting frogs can be found in my book, **Painting More Animals on Rocks**, (North Light Books, 1998.)*

Surrounded by smooth river rocks, the pebbled look of this fish pond seems perfectly natural.

Here is the first pond I ever painted. Re-sealing pond rocks yearly will keep them looking fresh.

This moss lined "pocket pond" was painted on a natural rock about the diameter of a dinner plate. Seal the bottoms and sides any time rocks will be set into the ground.

Natural field stone, river rocks, and even bricks, can be used to surround a faux fish pond, hiding the edges and acting as a frame. Add a few flowering plants and turn a corner of your patio or deck into a small oasis.

A low rock wall serves as a backdrop for this pond.

For larger areas, consider combining several painted stones to make a bigger pond. Bridge the gaps with the same rocks used to surround the outer edges.

83

Basking Iguana

Give your garden a tropical accent when you make this life-like looking iguana that appears to be sunning itself atop a stone. Use a manufactured Pavestone®, available at garden centers and home improvement stores, a natural field stone, or even a large river rock. Surround your iguana with cactus or other plants to create a stunning tableau for your yard or patio.

Supply List

- *Pavestone Sandstone System™ Patio Stone in the shape shown*
- *Poster board for template*
- *Pencil*
- *1/2" utility brush*
- *Loew-Cornell Filbert brush Size 6*
- *Loew-Cornell Liner brush Size 0 or 1*
- *DecoArt Patio Paints in:*
    Citrus Green
    Cloud White
    Patio Brick
    Sprout Green
    Wrought Iron Black
    Sunshine Yellow

See pattern pages 110, 111 and 112

1 Transfer the Pattern

If you choose the same manufactured patio stone that I used, it will be simple to apply this design. Piece together the pattern provided and create a sturdy template on poster board. You may need to re-size the template for use on a natural stone. Place the template on a clean rock that has been washed and allowed to dry. Use a pencil to draw around it.

85

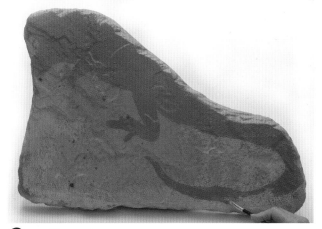

2 Fill in the Base Coat

A coat of Kilz oil-based primer should be applied first, covering the lizard shape only, to prevent flaking. Base coat the entire iguana with Citrus Green Patio Paint or exterior latex paint in lime green. Work it into any bubble holes or other irregularities. Use a small brush for the feet.

3 Draw on Details

Using the pattern as a guide, draw on the features, wrinkles, and other details with an ordinary pencil.

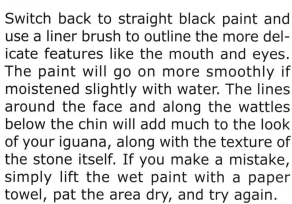

4 Paint Shadows, Outlines & Other Dark Details

Shadows beneath the iguana enhance the illusion of dimension. Begin with black paint, narrowly outlining the legs and the line below the chin, neck, body, and tail, with either a filbert brush turned sideways or a liner brush. Add a long curved nail to each toe. Soften the black paint by adding dark brown and just enough water to make the paint slightly transparent and widen the shadowed areas as shown. Shadows are widest under the body and along the fringed texture at the chin. Make them more narrow around the toes and below the back foot and tail. The shadow extends out below the tail.

Switch back to straight black paint and use a liner brush to outline the more delicate features like the mouth and eyes. The paint will go on more smoothly if moistened slightly with water. The lines around the face and along the wattles below the chin will add much to the look of your iguana, along with the texture of the stone itself. If you make a mistake, simply lift the wet paint with a paper towel, pat the area dry, and try again.

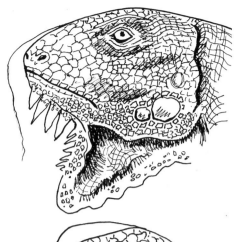

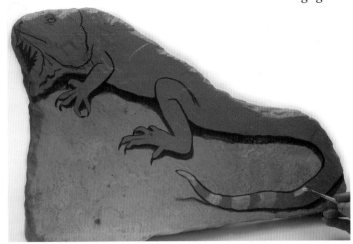

5 Paint Light Stripes on Tail

Use a clean filbert brush and white paint to add white stripes along the tail. These stripes should not look too solid, so add water as needed to allow some of the green paint below to show through. Make the stripes thicker as the tail widens out, with the last stripe ending behind the back leg.

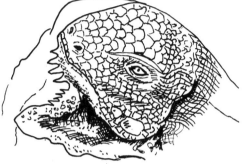

Face details for front & side views

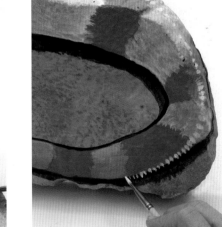

6 Add More Light Details to Head, Spine, & Tail

Use white paint to define the top of the lizard's face above the eye. Highlight a line above the mouth, fill in the two large scales on the cheek, and also fill in the fringe below the chin and the smaller fringe along the wattles. Outline underneath the wattles as well.

Begin a row of short, slanted spine lines just behind the head, following a line along the center of the back and then curving with the tail.

As the tail narrows, the spines should grow smaller so that they end up being splinter-like before disappearing altogether by the time you reach the fifth white section up from the tail tip.

7 Paint Lightened Skin Tones

Mix Patio Brick and Sunshine Yellow 1:3, then add enough white to get a color similar to the swatch below. Pick it up with a dry filbert brush and wipe most away so that the rest must be scrubbed on to the tops of the front and rear leg and along the front of the wattle.

Skin Color Swatches

Base Color *Shadow Color* *Highlight Color*

8 Create Shadows & Creases

Add a touch of Patio Brick to Sprout Green to get an olive green color. Use a damp filbert brush to shadow along the underside of the iguana, and to soften the black outlines on the head. Use the pattern as a guide in placing shadows on the legs, around the eye, and on the face. Along the torso and back, add shadows to suggest creases and folds in the skin. Also use this color to shadow the bottom and around the edges the spines so they stand out.

9 Extend Shadows Along Tail

Use the same dark green color to shadow the length of the tail to where it curves. Switch to the lower side of the tail and continue down to the tip. Leave a narrow line of light paint uncovered along the very bottom edge in contrast to the shadow below.

10 Cross-Hatch Texture Along Tail

Switch to a liner brush and white paint to make delicate cross-hatching that suggests the texture of scales along the bottom edge of the tail. Loosen the paint with water so that it flows off the tip of the brush to create these delicate lines.

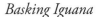

11 Fill in Tiny Facial Scales

Still using a liner brush and white paint, begin adding small flecks along the wattle and under the neck and chest. Extend a white line along the belly. Add enough Citrus Green to the white to make a pale green and use it to extend the scale pattern over the jowl, fitting the scales together like a mosaic, with larger pieces around the two existing scale shapes.

12 Paint Underside & Add Highlights

Widen the white outline from the chest along the belly with a dry filbert brush, feathering the edges upward. Add a touch of Citrus Green to white paint and use a dry filbert brush to apply soft highlights along the topmost curve of the front and back legs. Highlight a swath along the cheek below the eye, then add highlights along side the shadows to play up the creases at the neck and along the body as shown.

13 Create Scale Textures on Head

Give the iguana realistic texture by using a clean liner brush, and the same mix of green and brown, to cover the head with scales that fit together like a mosaic. Outline around the scales lined up along the mouth. The nose and forehead scales are larger, then get smaller below and behind the eye. Extend the pattern across the top of the head, but leave an area behind the eye unpainted.

14 Paint Transitional Scales

The area behind the eye forms a transition from the mosaic-style scales to a kind of wavy cross-hatching. Curve the lines to suggest the underlying shape of the head, and let your brush tip wobble a bit so that the pattern is not overly uniform.

15 Extend Cross-Hatching Along Body

Continue to paint narrow lines that curve and dip, accentuating the underlying rumples of the skin. Use the guidelines on the pattern as inspiration, but don't worry about copying them exactly. These lines will add subtle texture and do not have to be perfect. On the front leg, curve the lines to suggest the rounded shape. Let the lines become thin and faint as they extend down the fingers.

16 Texture for Rear Leg

Paint the scale texture on the rear leg starting at the knee and working back along the thigh. Below the knee, gently change the angle to transition the cross-hatching to follow the shape of the lower leg.

17 Texture Along Tail

Add diagonal, cross-hatched lines along the lower half of the tail, stopping short of the light scale texture painted earlier. As before, follow the tail to where it bends, then drop down to the lower half.

18 Paint Tiniest Scales

Moisten the paint so that it flows smoothly from the brush tip to create a very fine, delicate webbing of scale textures along the upper portion of the spiky white wattles at the chin.

19 Integrate Highlights

Extend the tips of the cross-hatched lines so that they overlap slightly into the highlighting along the ridge above the iguana's eye. This is a small touch, but adds to the realistic look.

20 Highlight Selected Scales

Switch to white paint with just a touch of Citrus Green added. Use a liner brush to make a lighter set of cross-hatching along the wrist and the top of the front foot. Also dot this color into the centers of several rows of cross-hatching along the upper edge of the arm above the elbow.

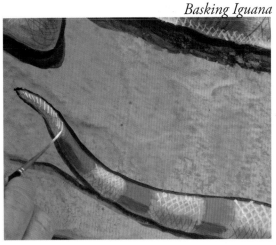

21 Add Texture with Highlights

Use pure white paint, loosened to go on smoothly, to create cross-hatched texture along the top edges of the tail's lighter sections. Don't overlap the dark outlines which define the shape of the tail.

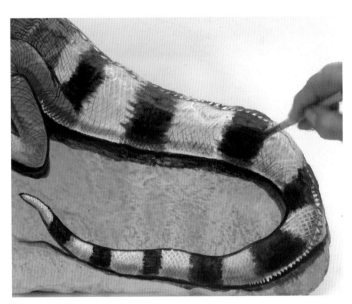

22 Paint Dark Tail Stripes

Mix enough black into a small amount of Patio Brick paint to create a deep brown shade. Use a filbert brush to stroke it into the spaces between the white stripes along the center of the tail. Turn the filbert brush sideways and give the edges slightly ragged-looking texture.

23 Paint Eye Details

Fill in the eye with solid Patio Brick, then add a trace of black to darken it and paint a shadow below the curve atop the eye. Let the paint dry before adding a black pupil to the center of the eye, placing it so that it seems to hang from the top of the eye.

24 Paint Nail Details

A narrow line of white along the top of each curving nail will give them a soft gleam.

25 Last White Touches

Two tiny specks of white, one on either side of the pupil, make the eye look wet. Also use white to brighten the edges of the spikey wattles below the chin to make them stand out.

26 Lighten the Eyelids

Add a trace of Citrus Green to white paint and use the tip of a liner brush to surround the eye with narrow lines that help to frame this important feature.

27 Add Brown Shades

Transparent touches of reddish-brown warm the skin and add visual interest. Use Patio Brick watered down to a transparent wash. Dab and blend a bit of this color into the corner in front of the eye, then add another swath of it below the back corner. Since iguanas tend to have somewhat mottled skin, touches of this color can be applied to the upper portions of the front and rear legs and perhaps behind the head among the creases there. Use a tissue to blot the paint for a very understated effect.

28 Create Soft Gleams Along Tail

Pick up a small amount of white paint on the tip of a filbert brush, and wipe away any excess, then use the remaining pigment to create a line of soft highlights down the length of the tail. These will show mainly in the dark segments.

More Ideas

Iguanas can also be painted on natural stones. Look for rocks that have enough height to allow the tail to curve around the base. A rock that narrows to a ridge along the top will add to the illusion that the lizard is actually basking upon it.

Combine a basking iguana with a faux fish pond for a truly dramatic nature scene.

Index

Hooked on painting rocks?

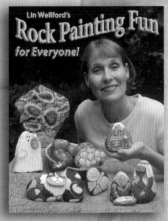
ArtStone Press
0-9777065-0-8

Lin's other books and video show how easy it is to transform ordinary rocks into an amazing variety of three-dimensional art works!

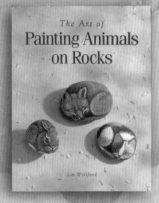
North Light Books
0-89134-572-8

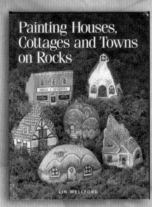
North Light Books
0-89134-720-8

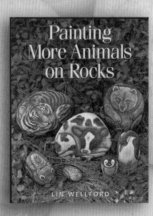
North Light Books
0-89134-800-X

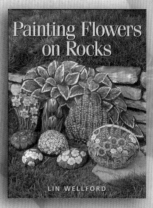
North Light Books
0-89134-945-6

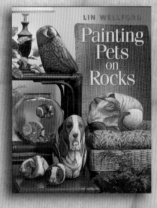
North Light Books
0-58180-032-0

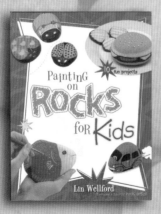
North Light Books
1-58180-255-2

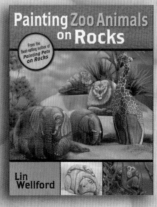
North Light Books
1-58180-465-2

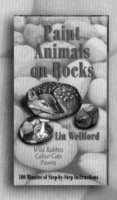
ArtStone Press
0-9700713-0-2

Autographed copies are available through Lin's website, www.LinWellford.com.
Books are also sold in retail book stores and many craft and hobby outlets.
Most titles can be purchased by calling North Light Books, (800)289-8963.
See the following page for complete information on ordering by mail.

Rock Painter's Resources

The supplies needed for painting rocks are common and should be easy to find. If you are unable to locate products in your area, contact the manufacturers listed below for help finding a local retailer.

Brushes
Loew-Cornell, Inc.
400 Sylvan Avenue
Englewood Cliffs, NJ
07632
(201) 836-7070
www.loew-cornell.com

Paints
DecoArt Patio Paint
P.O. Box 386
Stanford, KY 40484
www.decoart.com

Manufactured Stone
Pavestone Company
Corporate office
(817) 481-5802
www.pavestone.com

Liquid Nails
925 Euclid Avenue
Cleveland, OH 44115
www.liquidnails.com

More Resources

Yahoo Web Group:
Meet other rock painters
on-line at this free club:
www.groups.yahoo.com/
group/rockpainting

Rock Art News
Sign up for Lin's free
E-newsletter at:
www.LinWellford.com

Mail Order Information

Painted Garden Art Anyone Can Do (112 pages) _____ $ 22.99 (Plus postage—

Rock Painting Fun for Everyone! (96 pages)_____ $ 19.99   see below)

Painting on Rocks for Kids (64 pages)_____ $ 12.99

The Art of Painting Animals on Rocks (130 pages) _____ $ 22.99

Painting Houses, Cottages and Towns on Rocks (130 pages)_____ $ 22.99

Painting More Animals on Rocks (130 pages) _____ $ 22.99

Painting Flowers on Rocks (130 pages) _____ $ 22.99

Painting Pets on Rocks (130 pages)_____ $ 22.99

Painting Zoo Animals on Rocks (130 pages)_____ $ 22.99

Paint Animals on Rocks with Lin Wellford (Video) _____ $ 15.95

Postage on any one item is $2.75; for two or more items, add $2.00 each.
(Prices subject to change—if they go up, you will be contacted.)

Mail to: ArtStone Press, 9328 Hwy. 62 E, Green Forest, AR 72638

Painted Garden Art Project Patterns

Most of the patterns on the following pages are sized to fit the materials indicated for them in the individual chapters. They do not need to be enlarged or adjusted. Scan or trace the image on each page, then transfer it directly onto the stone using transfer or carbon paper, or transfer onto card stock or poster board to create and cut out a reusable template.

The Butterfly Stepping Stone pattern is one half of the complete design. Make one copy, then reverse or flip over the pattern to make the second half. The patterns for the diagonal and square stepping stones are 1/3 of full size and will need to be re-sized to create a full-size, twelve-inch template.

Elephant pattern

Baby elephant pattern for
corner piece

Frog pattern for scalloped border

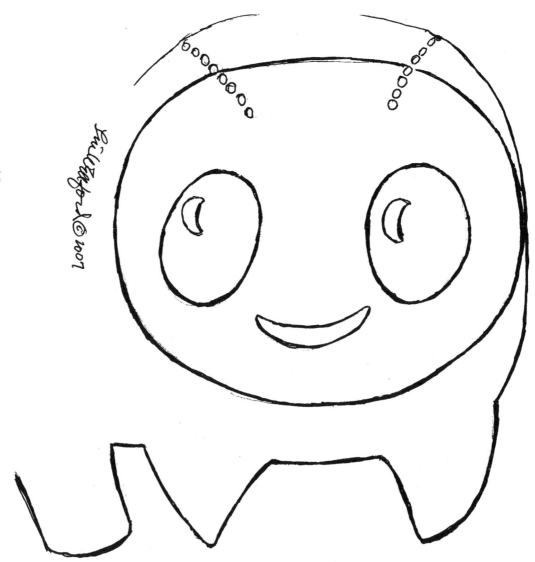

Caterpillar head pattern

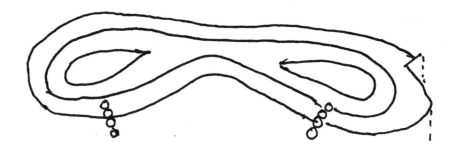

Caterpillar head pattern
top view

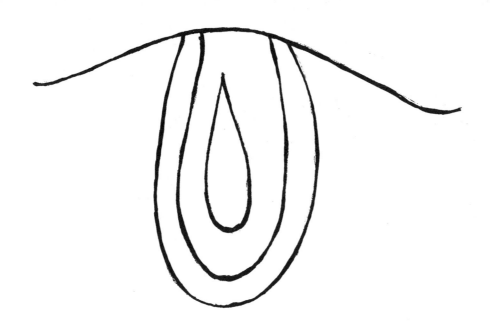

Caterpillar
body segments

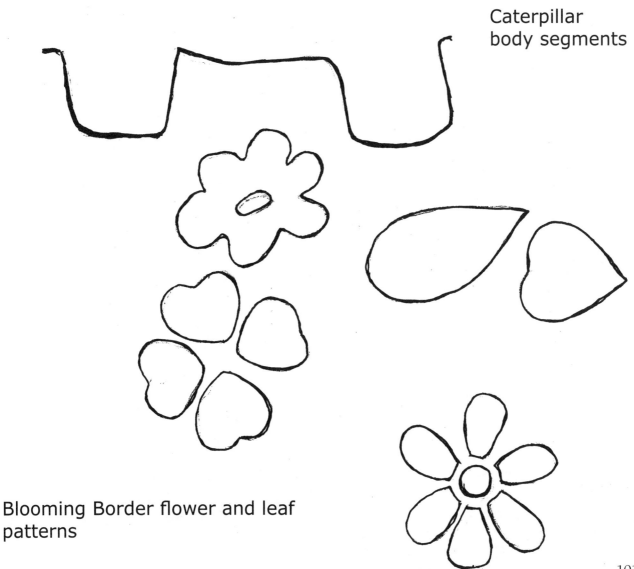

Blooming Border flower and leaf
patterns

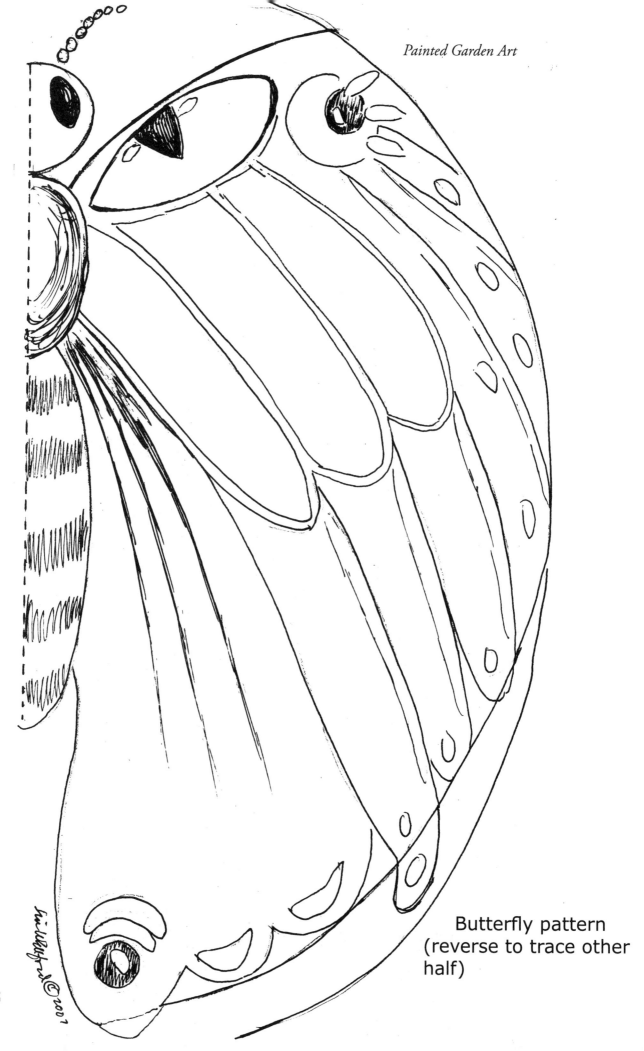

Butterfly pattern
(reverse to trace other
half)

Butterfly Stepping Stone patterns— diagonal and square designs

Stone Planter pattern for left half

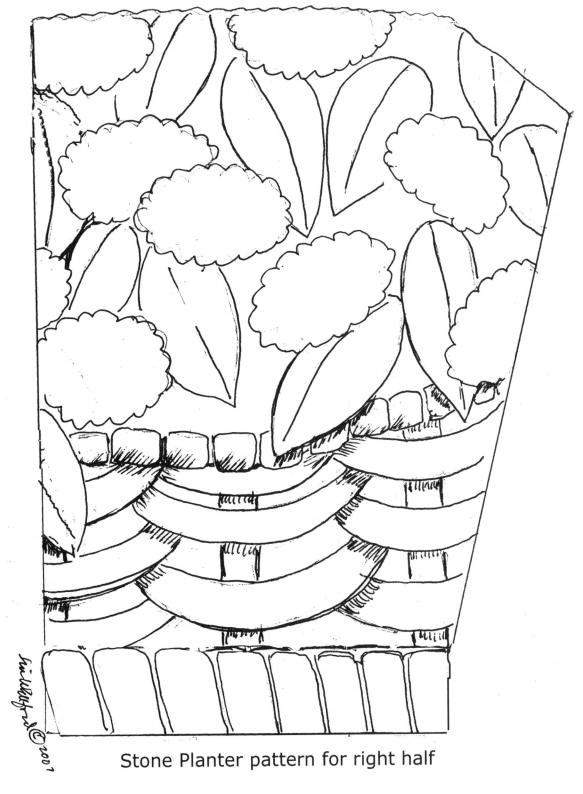

Stone Planter pattern for right half

Stone Planter pattern for top left
side

Stone Planter pattern for top right
side

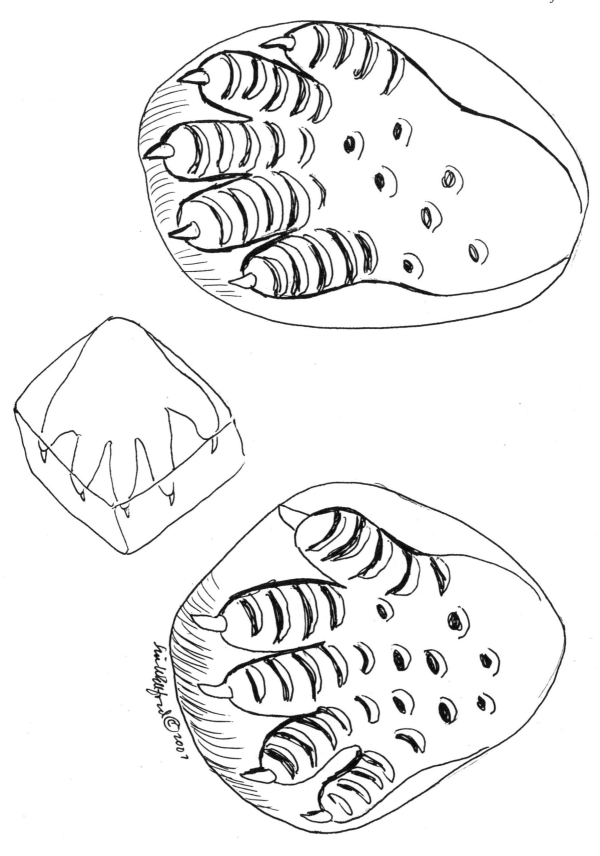

Front and back Garden Gator feet plus layout example for foot on
manufactured square brick

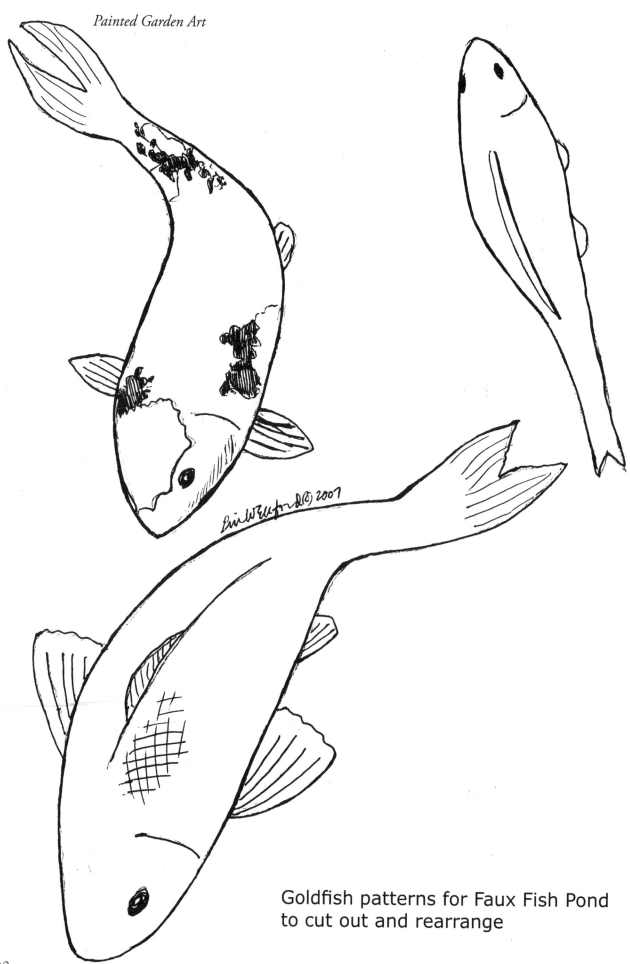

Goldfish patterns for Faux Fish Pond
to cut out and rearrange

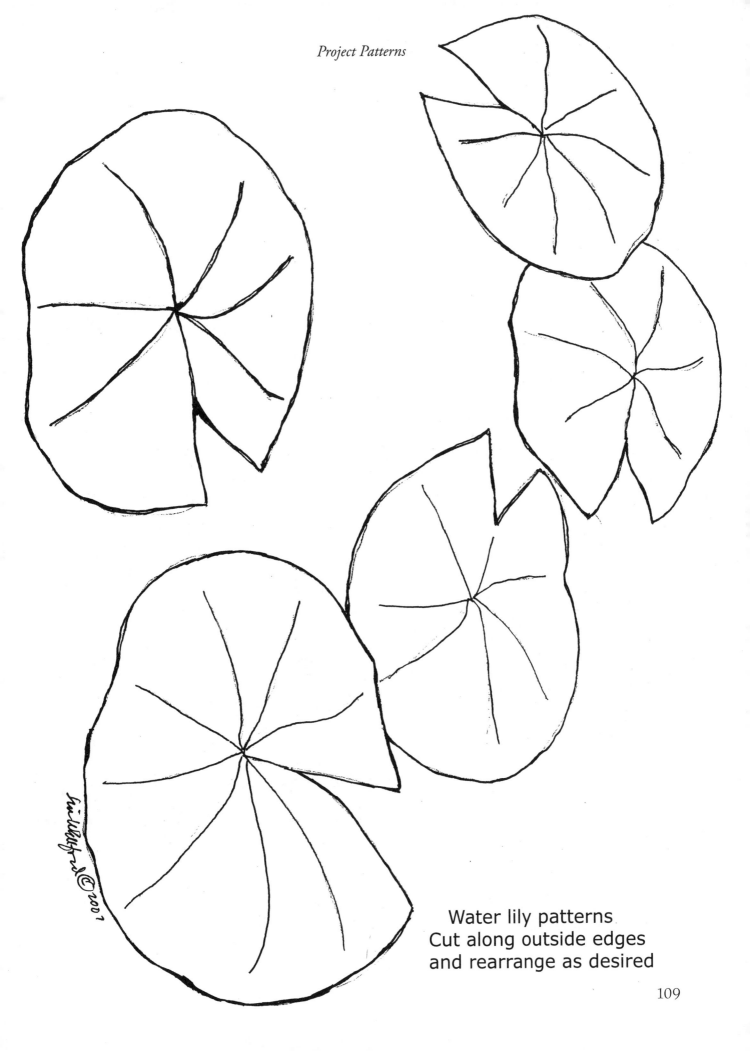

Water lily patterns
Cut along outside edges
and rearrange as desired

Basking Iguana Pattern—Head

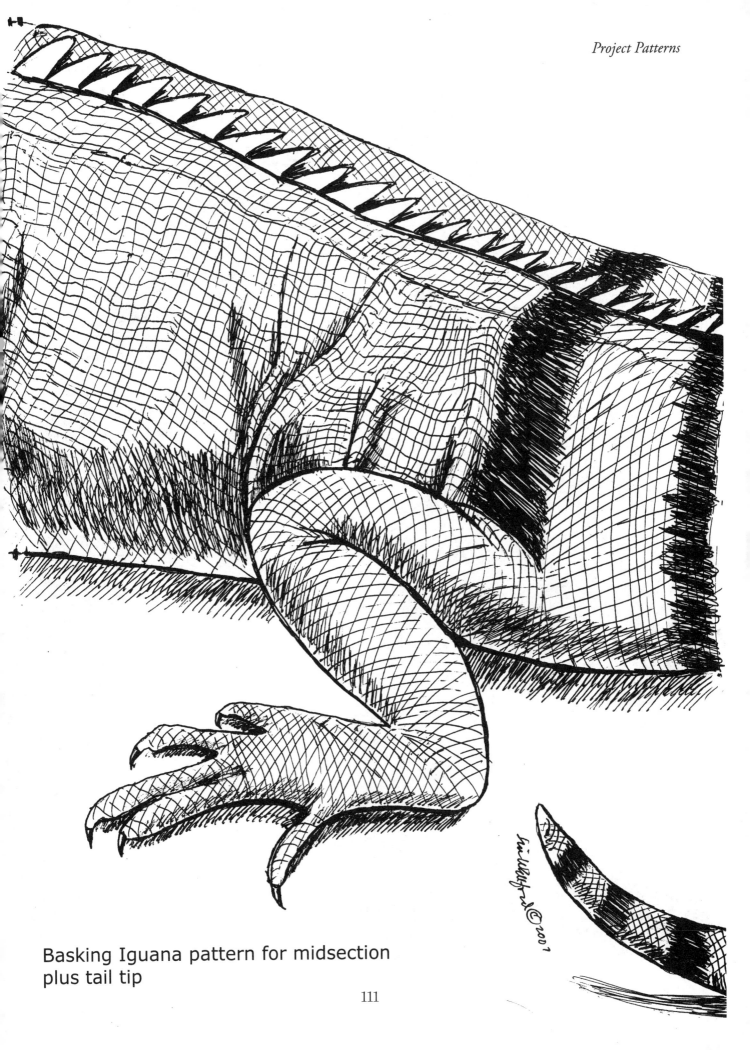

Basking Iguana pattern for midsection
plus tail tip

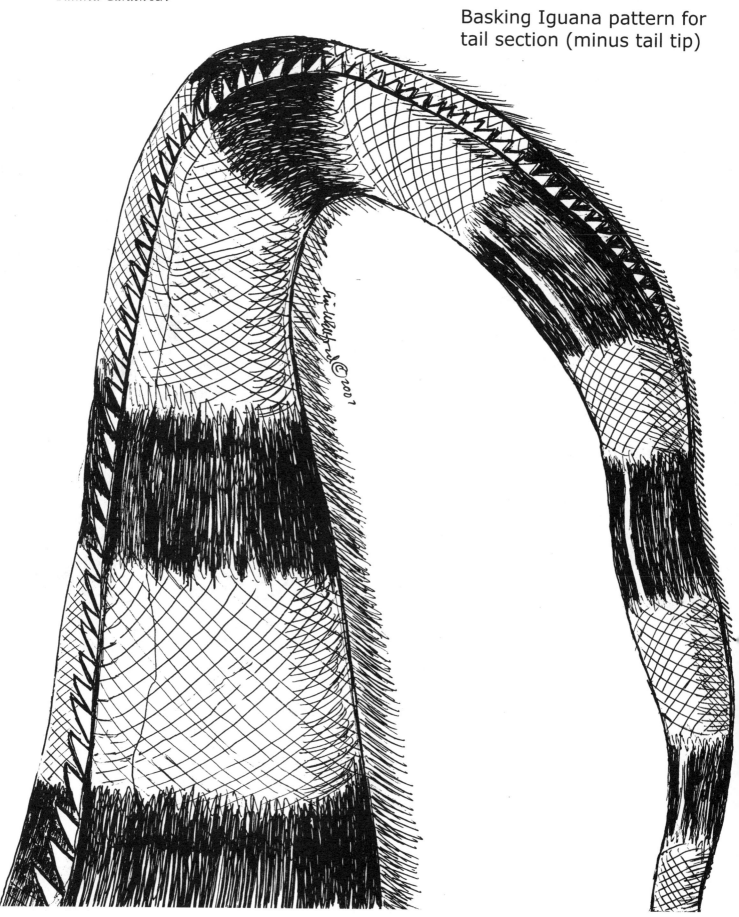